YOUR TEENA(
1 DIABETES DIAGNOSIS

One parent's honest guide to survival

YOUR TEENAGER'S TYPE 1 DIABETES DIAGNOSIS: ONE PARENT'S HONEST GUIDE TO SURVIVAL

First edition. January 6, 2018.

Written by Sara Hickmott.

Sara Hickmott

INTRODUCTION:

Firstly, sincerely thank you for choosing this book among all the other choices out there. I know you had a lot of options, so I hope you will not be disappointed in picking our story to guide you through the parental challenges of your teenage child's diagnosis.

A couple of housekeeping pointers -

What this book won't do:

There are hundreds of books out there covering the medical aspects of dealing with and living alongside Type 1, but this book is not intended to be such.

My first advice would always be to speak to someone who knows your child's unique medical circumstances best. A professional.

What this book WILL do (if I've done my job well!):

In writing this honest and open account of our journey through diagnosis and onwards into 'normal life', I've focused more on the stuff no one really tells you about.

My aim is to give you a different picture, to share honestly the psychological dramas I've been through as a parent, and some of the emotional impact you should expect in the hope that you feel you're not alone in this lifelong journey.

Above all, I wish you and yours all the very best in your life alongside Type 1. After all, that is what it is all about – learning to live with, not fighting against, this lifelong condition.

PART 1: Our journey towards - and then reluctantly through - diagnosis:

<u>a.</u> <u>B.D (or, 'Before Diabetes').</u>

Life as a parent is amazing, scary, fulfilling, expensive (oh my goodness, yes!), and is also a constant source of worry. Even when your child is no longer technically a child but a young adult. I'm no exception, which is why I felt compelled to write this book.

Those fearful, sometimes irrational thoughts usually strike hardest with our first born. The very first 'worry' I had was really quite a weird one, and it started in pregnancy. It was not the usual type of worry about whether he or she might have a major birth defect, or disfigurement, or life-threatening illness, or even (god forbid) whether I would carry to term.

Oh no, the very worst my naïve 27-year-old brain could conjure was whether he/she would have all 10 fingers and toes! Not exactly up there with the most critically life-changing of events.

It seems odd now to think about that, in the context of where I am as a parent to the above-mentioned child now. Not in my wildest of nightmares could I have come up with Type 1 Diabetes (Diabetes Mellitus to give a rather grand name to an evil condition).

It's only thanks to a girl named Rebecca from my 4th form Geography class, that I had knew anything about Diabetes at all.

Rewind to approximately 1985 and the 4th form days of secondary school. I remember some of our year had gone away to France on a school trip, and it was during that trip that news got back that Rebecca was seriously ill in hospital. I don't think we all quite understood what it all meant when we were told she had diabetes, but I recall her being off school for ages.

When she eventually returned, I sat alongside her in class and watched with consternation as our lessons were quite literally punctuated the pricking of her finger to test her blood sugar levels. Things went back to normal for everyone else, but I now know just how much things were never going to be 'normal' for Rebecca or her family ever again.

Diabetes played no further part in my life, or that of anyone I knew, until the summer of 2015.

<u>a.</u>　<u>Denial - slow realisation - yet more denial:</u>

Fast forward to summer 2015 and the end of the first year of Sixth Form for my daughter.

This is where our normal family life began to unravel.

We are unwittingly being plunged into the unknown, to a place where life will never be the same again.

The first sign of something being wrong came during the April / May of AS- Levels, although symptoms were so slight as to almost go unnoticed:

There were the complaints of being desperate for the loo during lessons, despite having been regularly and not having drunk that much to justify it. The tiredness, the achy limbs. The sort of thing which could easily be put down to the weight of exam stress, or generally being in a teenage body which is always yawning, always hungry and always grumpy, right? Wrong.

[Note: for the benefit of readers for whom a diagnosis has not yet been made, www.diabetes.org.uk lists several common, though not exhaustive, symptoms as follows:

- Going to the toilet a lot, especially at night

- Being constantly extremely thirsty

- Feeling more tired than usual

- Losing weight without trying to

- Genital itching or thrush (including oral thrush)

- Cuts and wounds taking longer to heal

- Blurred vision]

A trip to the doctor came up with oral thrush, and a dose of antibiotics. No further investigations made for this previously thriving child who had barely had a single day sick in her 17 years to date.

Then things started to pick up again, or so it would seem, and the thrush got better. Or maybe we were just all getting used to physical and emotional symptoms which can so easily seem 'normal' when right under your nose every day. These symptoms didn't exactly come and go, but they became less obvious or at least less mentioned.

School and exams finished for the summer, and we went on a family holiday to Germany. Just before the trip I distinctly remember looking at my eldest in in the kitchen and saying, 'Look at you, skinny minny!'

What an irony that was. My daughter was not just slim, she was wasting away right under my very eyes but this still didn't really register with me as a problem or an issue.

During the holiday, being with her every day, I began to realise that her obvious lack of energy, her constant hunger, and many visits to the loo might perhaps be early symptoms of diabetes. I even mentioned it to my sister, who we were staying with. She dismissed it, but something kept nagging away in the back of my mind. Even though I was starting to think this could be the D-word, I don't remember being scared about it. That was all waiting for me in the coming months and years. I was still at the naïve stage. The somewhat blissful denial. The D-word. D for denial and D for diabetes.

One thing you need to know about my daughter, is that she isn't one to complain. She's not a lightweight who takes to her sick bed at the slightest niggle. In fact, growing up, I could count on the fingers of one hand the number of days off school she had. She was robust, and strong.

Perhaps part of me relied on this fact to push away any thoughts of serious illness. Maybe if she had been a sicklier child we might have concluded differently, and sooner. Maybe. If. Perhaps. No good getting the retrospectoscope out now!

During the early part of August I started to notice that she was drinking a lot more than would be considered normal, and she was still complaining of being tired. She called me from a day trip out with friends to say she'd been sick on the train home, so I went to collect her from the station rather than leaving her to walk as had been the original plan. Thinking it was a stomach bug, we all thought no more of it.

Now, putting these pieces together, I can see it must have been the start of ketoacidosis.

During that horrible week, she even went back to the doctor to get checked, and yet again ended up with a course of antibiotics to deal with the oral thrush which was still hanging about. I was busy with work (something which really haunts me now, I should have been more present, I should have......I should have.... the guilt...).

I went on a work trip to see a client and spent the whole day worrying myself silly about her, constantly checking up to see if she was ok. She said she was.

This was really the final turning point, because I had also started to notice that her breath smelled odd. Kind of like nail varnish remover, or pear drops. Of acetone. Which ironically is exactly what it is. The body, in trying to deal with ridiculously high levels of sugar in the blood, starts to kick out toxins into the breath, and this is what you can smell if you're as well-endowed in the nose department as I am. It's unmistakeable.

    a.   The diagnosis:

The very next day after that client visit I rang my work to tell them I was taking her to the doctor as I thought she had diabetes. I remember thinking, well it will be ok because she hasn't really got diabetes.

Deep down I must have known with more certainty than I was admitting, because when I spoke to the receptionist to book the appointment, I made sure they would see her immediately by telling them of my amateur diagnosis.

Sitting in that waiting room was the last 5 or 10 mins of our lives spent without diabetes (or B.D as it shall be known).

Without the confirmation of what I already knew in my heart was a fact. Even sinking into the neighbouring chair to my daughter in the doctor's surgery, I remember almost counting the seconds before the doctor would inevitably utter the words, 'I think you're right' after I'd made my amateur diagnosis out loud to ensure that we wouldn't be fobbed off again.

It felt like time had slowed down and almost stopped as the doctor carefully pricked my daughter's finger to check her blood sugar levels. She had already dipped the urine to note that there were indeed a very high level of ketones and protein present. This was something I'd not seen since my own diagnosis during pregnancy with pre-eclampsia. I was already counting down the seconds now until I heard the words I already knew were coming.

Finally, she turned around to face us from her position over by the sink and the sharps bin. Her face told me all I needed to know.

Next there was a quick phone call to the children's ward at the local hospital (quite funny really when you consider that at the time my daughter was 4 months away from her eighteenth birthday), the printing of a letter to take with us 'without delay', and the ushering out of the door to make way for the next patient to take our place in the long list of daily appointments. What I do remember from this picture engrained in my memory, is the (female) GP's obvious sympathy and concern for us, having just delivered some pretty damning news.

I don't remember exactly the sequence of events which followed, except to say that I called work to tell them what was going on and that I wouldn't be in that day.

Next I went to collect my 2 younger children from childminder as it was still the school summer break, and drove calmly and sedately (for once in my life!) up to the hospital, a 30 min drive away from where we live.

I must have known we were going to be in it for the long haul otherwise I wouldn't have felt the need to collect the younger ones so early. My husband would be back from work, but not until much later, and after the childminder's hours.

Such calmness and clarity of thinking is sometimes just what happens when you're faced with a stressful and unnerving situation. I can be the world's worst worrier about the tiniest of inconsequential details, but give me something major and I'll be all calm and business-like organisation.

The ward team was expecting us, having been called ahead by the GP, and we were all shown to a bed in the assessment area to wait for the next steps. I remember it being very quiet in the ward, and therefore couldn't quite make out why it seemed to take forever for someone to appear to check us in, with the usual questions about name, DOB, address etc.

The rest of it was a bit of a blur, and I couldn't say how long we waited to see the doctor, who came over with a deadly serious look on his face to deliver the news. At first when he said, 'I'm really sorry...but...' I thought he was going to say the C word. So, it was with an odd sense of relief (not the right word but in the relative context of the C word it kind of was) when he said, 'Your daughter has type 1 diabetes'.

And right there, the 3 months of slow realisation and denial was over. One second before, there was still a chance (a slim one, but still a chance) that it wasn't real. Now, one second later, there was no going back. Nothing would be the same again. Sounds hugely dramatic, but that's how it felt.

From there it was all wheels in full speed motion. We were quickly found a private room, and within the hour the diabetes specialist nurse (DSN) had been to visit. People say the NHS is slow and lumbering, but the speed at which things happened for us was impressive.

Armed with a whole plethora of printed material, some much needed insulin to start the immediate treatment, a very welcoming and sympathetic bedside manner and a little fluffy teddy sporting a blue JDRF T-shirt, our DSN was a lovely lady who very much helped us to deal with the situation in these early hours where everything was a bit of a blur.

Presumably you're reading this because you are in a similar situation yourself, so let me reassure you now that you will be given a LOT of information in a very short time. You will nod and try to smile, and you may even crack a joke or two (a knee-jerk reaction to the relief of a diagnosis in my case), but you will only absorb about 10% of what you're being told. If you make peace with that now you will save yourself a lot of stress later.

Because my daughter was almost 18 the team felt it imperative that she should administer her own injections right from the outset. This is a very important step in getting over any psychological barriers to treatment. In at the deep end. After all, as a young adult with a reasonable amount of independence, it's completely impractical for anyone other than your son or daughter to inject their insulin and check bloods on a day-to-day basis.

Whilst they need to learn to look after themselves very quickly as a matter (quite literally) of life and death, this is not to say they won't need your support and help for days when they don't cope well, or are ill. No-one is infallible, and we all need someone to just take over on the odd occasion.

This is the practical me speaking. Doesn't mean my heart didn't rip a little further from my chest to watch my daughter inject herself. It's hard. Very, very hard. More on the emotional impact of T1D later in the book. For now, we're talking actions, practicalities and the sequence of events.

I should also mention that my daughter's case is quite unusual in that she was reasonably 'clinically well'. A somewhat odd description for someone whose pancreas has packed its bags and headed for the coast. In reality what this means is, bluntly, most diagnoses are made when the person has already collapsed into a diabetic coma, or keto-acidosis. They don't usually come in via the GP, accompanied by their siblings and walking by themselves.

The consultant in charge was clearly impressed that I had managed to make my own diagnosis. He reckoned I had done very well for a non-medically trained person and I should be proud. "well done Mum" were his words.

I just remember feeling guilty that I hadn't spotted this horrible condition / disease even sooner. But there you go.

a. After hospital – the first days at home:

When I said, you get a lot of information thrown at you in a short space of time.... this certainly became evident immediately on leaving the safety blanket of the hospital.

Whilst on the ward, the DSN was never too far away and was on call to answer questions at any time. Leaving the hospital with my newly diagnosed diabetic daughter felt strangely reminiscent of leaving hospital with her some 17 years and 9 months earlier as a new-born. I felt the same strange sense of a void around us as I had all that time ago. The comfort blanket of the expert knowledge had vanished from our physical space, to be replaced by the expectation of standing on our own two feet, with backup and help either a phone call or an internet search away.

About the internet and all the glorious (and not so) information which is out there at our fingertips – we were told by the DSN under no circumstances to visit any sites for advice other than www.diabetes.org.uk[1] or www.jdrf.org.uk[2].

The power of Google can be awesome, but it can also be our worst enemy when seeking health advice. No wonder doctors hate it when they hear the words 'I googled it and....'!

Almost certainly they were trying to keep us from driving ourselves mad with all the super scary stories out there on the web. There are a million diabetes horror stories if you look for them hard enough. Negativity comes to find you very easily, especially when some deep-down part of you is actively looking for it.

Why do humans feel the need to catastrophize? This self-destructive behaviour is something I have perfected over the years as anyone who knows me will testify. Cheerful and positive on the outside but sometimes a quagmire of doom and gloom under the surface.

Those first few hours at home felt strange – as if the whole world had changed and nothing was recognisable any more. The anxiety and uncertainty of that first blood sugar check and insulin dose at home was peppered by self-doubt and worry that we might be doing it all wrong, at the wrong time.

It felt to me like my almost adult daughter was once again a small child, a fragile thing who could break at any time without warn-

---

1. http://www.diabetes.org.uk

2. http://www.jdrf.org.uk

ing. A kind of walking time-bomb made from the most delicate of glass.

At some point during that first day I remember breaking out of cool, calm and collected crisis management mode, and being hit like the proverbial brick by a huge tidal wave of emotion which seemed to come from nowhere and without warning. One minute I was fine, the next I was sobbing uncontrollably. This was shock of course. A delayed reaction following the previous 48 hours where everything moved so quickly that there was no time to think about anything much except getting through it.

I felt quite selfish behaving like this, as for my daughter it was of course a million times worse since it was her pancreas which had packed up, not mine. What I would have given to take the disease away from her and for me to have it instead. I was angry, I was fuming in fact that she should have this to deal with at an age where she had so much else to cope with in life. The transition through the final year of school, exams, and on to university. A whole life stretching out like a blank canvas, waiting for the first footprints of a path to forge itself. It was all so unfair!

As a parent, your instinct and very reason for being is to protect and nurture your child and pray that nothing bad ever happens to them. That's all you want, and you would do anything for them without question.

The emotional side of dealing with any illness will hit different people in different ways. Be under no illusion that it won't touch you.

Whether sooner, or much later, the PTSD (yes really) will catch up with you. Just be aware that It's coming so you can be as prepared as possible to deal with it. It might not show itself in any obvious way. There is no right or wrong way to react.

Back to the self-doubt and uncertainty. We must have read and re-read those leaflets given to us by the DSN a million times, looking for reassurance that the correct sequence of events in treatment was being followed. My child was looking to me for help, and for the first time I didn't have all the answers. Far from it. We must have called the hospital ward several times that day alone, even though it was the weekend, looking for any reassurance we could get that the world wasn't going to fall apart if my daughter inadvertently ate the 'wrong' thing at the 'wrong' time.

The first week at home followed a similar pattern, though it did gradually get easier with the practice of administering the treatment and the monitoring of blood sugars like clockwork. It felt like the whole day was dominated by dealing with this disease. There was no space in time or mind for anything else. The similarities with having your first child and the feeling of overwhelm this brings to your daily life is quite unnerving.

The DSN visited us at home on the Monday as we were 'released' from hospital over the weekend. I had taken some time off work to be with my daughter and her presence felt very reassuring after the freeform muddle of the weekend, much like the home visit from the midwife after you're set free into the world with a new born baby and no user manual!

I remember hovering around in the lounge like a spare part listening as the DSN and my daughter chatted about how she was getting on – it was 100% the right thing to do of course. No point in directing the conversation through me. It was clear my role as immediate caregiver had changed with the passing of the years. We were entering a new phase in the mother-daughter relationship dynamic.

The diabetes had pinpointed the demarcation line.

During that strange first week, where it felt like our world had been turned not only upside down, but inside out too, those regular visits from the diabetes team were both extremely welcome and reassuring. We had no idea that we would get so much intense and close attention (why would we? Never having had any direct experience of diabetes). We had not only the ear of the DSN, but also her team and a specialist nutritionist, who helped to guide the thinking and planning of meals and snacks. All of which is so important, if not critical, in the management of Type 1 diabetes.

My daughter seemed to be coping brilliantly with those first days. She was determined to get to grips with everything herself, rather than having things done for her or having to ask what to do every time. Although of course those occasions happened, becoming less frequent with each passing day, to my great pride.

The days immediately following a life-changing diagnosis are so often fuelled by practical matters, pushing out the psychological trauma to be dealt with later. This was true for both of us.

As exhausted as I was however, I found it incredibly hard to sleep at night. It was all relatively ok during the day when I had things to keep me occupied, stuff to do, etc. It's when I closed my eyes at night and was on my own in the dark, that the images and racing thoughts came at me like a battering ram, making it impossible to switch my mind off and get some much-needed rest.

I didn't want to leave her side, for fear she would die in the night and I wouldn't be there to save her. The knife-edge balance of this horrible condition loomed large in my mind, and I was convinced she would slip into a terrible hypo in her sleep and never wake up. I still sometimes have this fear, 2 years on. Perhaps I will never lose it, but I learn to live with it.

I assume this is a natural part of any parent's reaction, but I am also aware that I do tend to not only overreact to, but to catastrophize most health-related situations involving a loved one. I'll share this example with you to demonstrate just how extreme I can be - I remember once locking myself in my room as a small child, crying my eyes out because mum had hiccups and I was convinced she was going to die. Yes really. I'm not sure that's entirely normal, but it's taken me some 40 odd years to realise that I suffer with anxiety. I am coming to terms with that diagnosis and setting myself on the path to dealing with it now.

I am convinced that if my daughter hadn't been diabetic then neither of us would have taken steps to deal with the psychological condition we have both carried since childhood. My daughter too suffers anxiety, I am sure not just because of the diabetes. She was an anxious child too, but because some of her behaviour was just like mine when I was small, it didn't jump out at me as being obviously odd.

    a. <u>Getting back to (the new) 'normal':</u>

This will be the shortest section by far, since I'm not sure I even know what 'normal' is myself yet. Perhaps a new version of normal would be a more appropriate heading.

As if such a thing now exists! Life will become easier, but right now you will be reeling and it will all still be very raw and new.

At some point life will have to return to the everyday pattern of school and work. You may well have numerous other responsibilities to deal with, such as a partner, other children, other family commitments etc.

You will feel like a headless chicken, and if you're anything like me, your anxiety levels may sky-rocket at the very thought of leaving your diabetic child's side for the first time. This is all very normal, though nonetheless pretty distressing.

My best advice is to try to tell yourself that even though things will never be the same again, you will get used to this new version of life. Things will settle in time, and the sooner you can all get back to everyday routines, the better for everyone.

Remember that this is very much a grieving process, which typically goes something like this:

- Stage 1: Denial

- Stage 2: Anger
- Stage 3: Bargaining
- Stage 4: Depression
- Stage 5: Acceptance

To give you an idea of where I am in the process, I'd say around the early part of stage 5 right now, just over 2 years on from diagnosis.

I reckon that's not too bad considering, but bear in mind we are all individuals, so your own experiences will be just that, your own.

PART 2: Practicalities:

a. Prescriptions:

One of the first practical 'jobs' after leaving hospital is to visit the GP and make arrangements to get all the items needed on prescription. When we left the hospital, we were of course given a reasonable quantity of insulin pens, test strips, needles, glycogen treatments and the all-important item that every diabetic must come to hate because basically it screws up your fingers – the clicker needle to draw blood.

My advice with this would be never to assume that the GP knows anything about what is needed in terms of 'kit'. If there's one thing we've learned it's that pretty much no one except the DSN has a clue about Type 1. Get a list of things you must have from the DSN before the home visits end. Make sure you read it thoroughly and cross check against the supplies you have so you can be sure you know what is what.

> **Top tip:**
>
> Be prepared to argue with the GP about the number of test strips needed for a month's supply because it's REALLY important you don't run out. And you will ALWAYS use more than you think.

Our GP started us off with (as it turned out) only enough test strips to last a week as he assumed that bloods would only be checked a couple of times a day. Wrong. VERY wrong. In the early days, your child will probably be testing every hour or so, and obviously before meals to gauge the insulin needed. It's worth bargaining up front for using 10 strips per day as a minimum. They won't like it because test strips are EXPENSIVE – you'll find out if you ever run out and end up buying them in the pharmacy – they're about £30 for a small pot!

Also, it's worth assuming is that they will get the first prescription wrong. The GP requested the wrong needle size for the insulin pens, even though he was inputting from the DSN's list directly into the system. You probably won't realise as you will assume he or she knows what they're doing, until you go to fetch the scrip and find out it's all to cock.

Read the printed scrip before you leave the surgery to save yourself a lot of stress and hassle.

Finally, get the thing on managed repeat so you don't have to think ahead and put the scrip into the pharmacy 4 working days ahead of when you need it. This could just be a uniquely annoying quirk of our local health centre. Some are so advanced you can manage everything online.

I've deliberately steered clear of any specific medication details because everyone's regime is different. Just make sure you know what you need, roughly how much, and check, check, check. If in doubt, ask the DSN. They're an absolute treasure and your new best friend.

a. School/ college:

Assuming your child is at school and they've already been made aware, your next step is to make sure that you know the school's guidelines and procedures for dealing with diabetic children 'in loco parentis'.

Each school will be different and have their own policies, but it's worth asking how many members of staff are trained to deal with inevitable hypos / hypers, and where spare insulin supplies can be stored should a bag get lost or kit forgotten.

You may be lucky like me and have a super-organised, responsible and mature 17-year old, or you may have a 17-year old who is the complete opposite – can't help you with that one except to say that even the most diligently organised will forget their insulin and / or needles / finger pricker / test strips etc. on at least one occasion a month.

It happens and it's good to know where spares can be found.

There is nothing worse than receiving a panicked phone call from your child, or the school because of lost medication. Diabetes waits for no man, woman or child. It does its own thing and you can't delay treatment because it's not a convenient time.

If your child is sitting external exams such as GCSEs or A Levels, then check that the exams officer is aware of their condition as they should get special dispensation to have an exam stopped whilst they check their levels, eat or go to the toilet. Then make sure the exams officer informs the invigilators – my daughter had to go through the stress of having her blood sugar monitor be-ing taken away from her in the exam hall because the invigilator thought it was a mobile phone. Not all kids are great at shouting out a wrong judgement.

> **Top tip:**
>
> Be sure to find out the name, telephone number and email of the members of staff trained to deal with Type 1 and make sure you keep them updated with any changes to regime or medication as needed.

a.   Useful, essential and practical accessories:

Top of the list here is a **medical bracelet** to identify your child as a Type1 in case of emergency.

You can buy some nice styles online which look just like normal jewellery so your child doesn't feel like they're being 'tagged'!

We got ours from here: http://www.medicaltags.co.uk, but there's plenty of choice out there.

If your child is an insulin pen user then they will have numerous paraphernalia to cart around.

Something like a large compartment **pencil case** might be useful to keep everything safe and in one place.

> **Top tip:**
>
> All I can say to you is, get some form of ID. It can do no harm, and may save their life.

a. Telling friends, family and others:

This is such a personal issue, and your child will let you know how comfortable they feel with people knowing, and whether they want you to be open about their diagnosis or not. You are their parent of course, but if they're almost an adult then it's up to them. No need to take out an advert in the local paper (do people still do that?), or blast it all over social media.

Obviously, you will need to tell some people, not least should something happens to your child whilst in their company then they need to know how they can best help.

The essential people/ organisations on this list would be: School / College, immediate family (those living under the same roof), doctor and dentist.

It would also be wise for your child to mention to their employer if they have a part-time job. This is for their welfare, and should not be considered a means for any discrimination.

Close family members:

You'll need to run through the basics of what to do if your child is taken ill (essentially how to check their bloods, give insulin or hypo treatment if needed etc.) and can't help themselves. Anyone who lives in the same house will need to know, and even younger siblings should be aware so that they can read the signs and fetch help if they need to.

My daughter was good about sharing with her close friends (they knew anyway because, well, they're close), and once it was all out in the open they were keen to understand how they could help and what they should do if she was feeling unwell. A couple of them even took to carrying emergency Haribos in their bags just in case (though I'm pretty sure some were sneaked during lessons too!).

One friend even carried spare insulin and needles. There will always be that odd occasion when this essential kit gets left at home, especially during the first few weeks when new habits are being formed and there's so much to think about.

Not to put the onus on friends to be the carers in any way, but it will be a massive weight off your mind to know that someone is there to look out for your child when you're not with them. I know it certainly helped me to be less of a helicopter parent since this does no one any good.

Top tip:

Have hypo treatment in every corner, at home and at school so that there are always spares if needed.

To treat a hypo, eat or drink 15 to 20g of a fast-acting carbohydrate. This could be:

three glucose or dextrose tablets

five jelly babies

a small glass of a sugary (non-diet) drink

a small carton of pure fruit juice

a tube of glucose gel.

Above courtesy of www.diabetes.org.uk

a. Alcohol and socialising:

I won't lie, the first time my daughter went out 'socialising' (aka. drinking) with her friends, I was beside myself with worry. A little context – as I mentioned at the start of this book, she was 17, almost 18 when diagnosed, so the pub scene and, of course, alcohol had already been part of her life for a fair while.

If there's a worse time to become diabetic than just before your 18th birthday and your university years, I can't think of one.

The cruelty of the timing was not lost on us, as it came mere days before the obligatory teenage pilgrimage to the Reading Festival. Literally the weekend prior we were in hospital making a start on the treatment, still slightly in denial and kind of hoping that the 3-day sleep-deprivation, alcohol-fuelled mosh pit of a parental nightmare might still somehow be feasible.

The consultant looked quite shocked when the subject was broached, as if to say, 'Poor souls, they haven't quite grasped the situation'. Well no, I guess we hadn't, or maybe we had, but just didn't quite want to acknowledge defeat (and the loss of the £300 odd ticket....!)

Alcohol and diabetes aren't really the very best of friends it's fair to say, but on the positive side, for us it hasn't been quite the kiss of death (if you'll excuse the phrase) that we thought it might be.

Whilst it's never a good idea to drink to excess, for anyone of any age or medical history, my worst fears of a wine-induced coma after only a couple of glasses were somewhat a creation of my over-active imagination.

I have a black belt in worrying. Weapons-grade catastrophizing abilities.

Whilst other parents are worrying what mischief or danger their child might get themselves into from drinking, it's never really on the scale of the parent of a diabetic who really does have grounds for being that little bit more anxious.

Rest-assured your child will plan to be sensible, and most of the time they probably will be. However, there will always be that one occasion where it all goes out of the window and they get absolutely trashed. (NYE 2015 in our case).

I warn you now, this will happen so best to be prepared.

The phone call which came at around 1130pm from her best friend, who thankfully had the good sense to call me, was the worst experience ever. I must have broken the speed limit to drive the 7 miles into town to collect her. I was told she had passed out, so I really thought the worst and was in a proper panic by the time I arrived at the house party.

Luckily the part of my brain which was still functioning reasonably kicked in, and I managed to check her bloods whilst she was puking into a Tupperware bowl.... Basically, this anecdote ends with me spending the entirety of NYE / New Year's night setting an alarm on the hour every hour to check her bloods to make sure she wasn't coming down too quickly from the high glucose levels brought on by the wine.

Alcohol will do that by the way, depending on the type you drink and your child's individual metabolism. It will send them high initially, then they'll come crashing down a few hours later – sometimes people wake up from sleep hypos, but if they're off their **** then they're way less likely to.

Top tip:

The best advice I can give you is to let them find their own pace with drinking. If they're sensible they will manage themselves well and learn to incorporate the social aspects of drinking with living alongside the diabetes.

---

a. Travelling /overseas holidays and flying:

Aside from the ill-fated Reading Festival, the 2nd and final pressured year of A-Levels put a dampener on any travelling, save for a couple of weekends away. During these occasions, I had to try hard to turn down the worry-radar since it wasn't feasible for me to trail her around like a lost puppy (much as I wanted to).

It wasn't until the summer after A-Levels, and almost a year post-diagnosis, that I completed my PHD in worry management by seeing her off on a 10-day inter-railing trip with her friends.

This trip would cover numerous European countries and cities in a short time, all by rail (aside from the initial plane trip to Amsterdam to start the first leg). I think the months leading up to this trip of a lifetime must have been underpinned by a current of simmering worry for me as her mum.

The trip was so well-deserved, not least because it marked the end of school and the tough A Level curriculum. She had made me so proud in handling the first year of diabetes so well, but here I was wishing the trip would be cancelled for the purely selfish reason that I didn't think I could cope with her not only being away for 10 days, but worse, being abroad - without adults (which was in itself funny because she was 18 by then!), on a sleep-deprived, alcohol-fuelled trip of a lifetime.

How very dare she leave me at home to an almost certain fate of sleepless nights and constant monitoring of the mobile phone for any small signs of distress. Let me tell you, living in a heightened state of panic and worry without immediate and reasonable cause is very tiring and does you no good whatsoever.

Needless to say, the trip went well and she arrived home having had a wonderful time, and having been well looked after (when needed) by her amazing group of friends.

From a practical point of view there are a few things which it's useful to be prepared for when going away on holiday:

> 1) Flying: always, always put insulin and kit in hand luggage and don't let anyone tell you otherwise. Insulin in the hold where temperatures are freezing, means non-working insulin. Need I say more.
>
> 2) Also flying: make sure there's a note from the hospital or GP on headed paper stating the condition and

that medicine needs to be carried on the person at all times. Some airlines may wish to see evidence of the need for needle use, especially in the current climate. Although I must say, we have never been either asked or challenged either at security check or on board.

3) Take plenty of spare kit. More than you think will ever be needed in the time away. And consider giving an essential quantity to a travel companion just in case of lost / stolen bags.

4) Travel insurance – obviously essential from the medical point of view. Don't forget to mention the diabetes. I know, it sounds silly and obvious, but it can easily be forgotten until a seasoned travelling pro.

5) If visiting a hot country, consider buying a cool-pack to carry insulin as hot weather can make the insulin less effective. It needs to be stored in a fridge ideally, and if you're visiting (for example), Spain in the height of summer, you'll need to make sure the day's supplies whilst out and about are well protected against the searing 40-degree heat.

6) Take a copy of the prescription, just in case more supplies are needed whilst away.

7) Encourage your child to learn the basic words of a diabetic's language in the native tongue, e.g.: 'I'm diabetic' or 'I need insulin', and if you're going along too – learn yourself!

8) Be aware that being out of routine may make your child's bloods a little erratic. They may be higher than usual being in a hot climate, so they will need to compensate, which means more insulin, which means accounting for that in the supplies they take.

Top tip:

Plan, plan, plan like a ninja. Then check your plans again. Your efforts will be well-rewarded in minimised hassle and worry whilst away.

PART 3: Dealing with the emotional impact on you and your family:

a. PTSD – yours and theirs!

Sounds a bit dramatic, I know, and we touched on this a little earlier in the book briefly. It's a term you hear bandied around a lot, but more usually in an armed forces context, e.g. war veterans, or the police.

However, it's good to try to understand a little more about how this horrible condition might affect you so you can be prepared, or if not prepared then at least aware.

(Of course, PTSD affects your child too, but as this book is about you, the parent, that's where we will focus).

So, what's the definition of PTSD? According to the leading UK Mental Health Charity, MIND:

"PTSD is a type of anxiety disorder[1] which you may develop after being involved in, or witnessing, traumatic events. The condition was first recognised in war veterans and has been known by a variety of names, such as 'shell shock'. But it's not only diagnosed in soldiers – a wide range of traumatic experiences can cause PTSD[2]".

---

1. https://www.mind.org.uk/information-support/types-of-mental-health-problems/anxiety-and-panic-attacks/anxiety-disorders/

2. https://www.mind.org.uk/information-support/types-of-mental-health-problems/post-traumatic-stress-disorder-ptsd/causes-of-ptsd/

And the causes are many and varied, not least restricted to the following:

- a serious accident such as a car crash
- being violently attacked
- being raped or sexually assaulted
- being abused, harassed or bullied
- being kidnapped or held hostage
- traumatic childbirth[3], either as a mother or a partner witnessing a traumatic birth
- extreme violence or war, including military combat
- seeing other people hurt or killed
- surviving a terrorist attack
- surviving a natural disaster, such as flooding or an earthquake
- **being diagnosed with a life-threatening condition**
- losing someone close to you in particularly upsetting circumstances
- any event in which you fear for your life.

Having a child diagnosed is very shocking, scary, and can be overwhelming. In addition to the shock of the diagnosis (and even if you think you saw it coming as I did), the feelings don't go away after you've left the hospital. There is always fear and worry due to the nature of the disease. And even if you're not directly administering the insulin and immediate medical care that you would for a small child, dealing by proxy with low and high blood sugars, DKA, and the various medical decisions your child

---

3. https://www.mind.org.uk/information-support/types-of-mental-health-problems/

postnatal-depression-and-perinatal-mental-health/ptsd-and-birth-trauma/

is making for themselves on an hourly basis can sometimes be even worse.

There is the lack of control element. The 'are they doing it right' doubts, the 'Are they taking proper care of themselves' questions rattling around your head constantly.

Yes, it's probably also true that you're more likely to be affected by PTSD if you've previously experienced anxiety, depression or chronic stress. This is certainly part of my own back- story so I wasn't at all surprised when I started to have 'flashbacks' to the hospital ward (triggered by the smell of the insulin I can pick up when my daughter changes her insulin pod!), and feelings of dread and fear if she didn't answer a text by return.

In my wild imagination, she was collapsed in a coma somewhere and I would be getting a phone call or visit from the police to our family home at any moment. Horrible enough to experience in isolation, but when it happens on a daily basis and you realise you're living in a constant hyper-vigilant state, then it's maybe time to get some professional help.

Being the parent of a T1 young adult is of course different than being the parent of a dependent child with T1. You're that little bit removed from the situation yet the emotional burden is as heavy, and you would not be human if you didn't wish with all your heart that you could take this life-threatening condition away from your baby.

Truth is, no one can, but you can learn to live alongside type 1 if you understand and know yourself well and are prepared to act as soon as things become overwhelming.

Talk to your DSN and see if you can attend a course for parents of T1 children. Ask them if they can spare half an hour to talk to you about the realities of the disease if you want to get a good handle on the medical realities. But please don't Google stuff. That's rule #1. You'll only add to your stress and anxiety that way!

a. Anxiety and depression:

PTSD, anxiety and depression are close cousins, and since being diagnosed with a life-changing / threatening condition is a significant risk factor in the affected person developing one or more of the above, is it also possible that a parent of a child with such a condition could also suffer? I would strongly argue it is.

Even if you've never suffered from anxiety or depression before, it would be wise to keep checking in with yourself on this one as you come through the first year of your child's diagnosis. Lots of changes and adaptations will be made in the first months, and it's so easy to get caught up in the practical side of daily management, even if by proxy, that you may not realise that unhealthy habits and thoughts are creeping in.

Whilst I've always been a reasonably chilled out sort of parent (I think!) at least in comparison to a lot of parents I know, there is a small part of me prone to a little catastrophizing now and then. This took me a little by surprise when this really started to grow and take hold almost without any warning, and pretty quickly too after my daughter's diagnosis.

It all started with me being terrified to leave her during the day to go back to work. I was lucky to have a fairly understanding boss who allowed me to work from home. Nonetheless, I was even too anxious to leave her alone in a room without constant supervision. Writing this now, it sounds bonkers, but more of this in the next section about helicopter parenting.

When I eventually did return to the office, I was in such a state of high alert that I could barely concentrate or take my attention away from my phone in case I missed an urgent or desperate call for help.

By the way, I'm still not good with leaving my phone unattended, but I am at least now learning to manage it a little better than before because to be quite honest, my anxiety levels were reaching such a height that it was becoming unmanageable and was beginning to interfere with my sleep too.

There are plenty of studies which will tell you that all of the above is 'normal' for the parent of a diabetic child, but whilst it certainly helps to know you're not alone (and this is a major reason why I wanted to write this book), you still need to find a way to come through it with your sanity intact. Now I'm not saying for one minute that you can 100% come through the other side and suddenly wake up one morning 'cured' of your diabetes-related anxiety – if only it were that simple – what I am saying is be alert to your state of mind, act on any negative feelings as quickly as possible by whatever means necessary.

For example, you may find that joining a Facebook group for parents of children with Type 1 will help. For me, it just made everything a whole lot worse because (and this is meant with kindness), there's always someone with a catastrophic story out there and you REALLY don't need to be reading that at 2am when you can't sleep because you're wired with anxiety.

You could talk to your child's DSN about your feelings and worries, they might be able to recommend a support group, some reading, or a course you could go on to manage your specific diabetes-related anxieties.

Unfortunately, for me the anxiety got so out of hand that I ended up at the doctors after having pretty much a nervous breakdown over a work-related issue (turns out the work thing was just the proverbial 'straw'). To cut a long story short however I am happy to say that I am working through some of these issues with the help of my GP and through other lifestyle techniques (not least my new passion for running), and am now much better at managing my anxieties around my daughter's illness.

I use the word 'manage' very specifically because I don't believe I am going to be 'cured' of anxiety. All I can do is to be kind to myself and learn to be a less anxious parent to my now adult child.

a. Helicopter parenting:

The term helicopter parenting originally referred to someone who keeps a close watch and control over their child's achievements and progress, putting extreme pressure on them to perform and do well.

You'll forgive perhaps my slightly skewed use of the term here, because what I'm referring to is nothing to do with achievements, and everything to do with being over-present in my daughter's daily life. Hovering over her like a helicopter in case something bad might happen. Of course, I know it's irrational and if something bad was going to happen, it would do so regardless of my presence. As if I were some kind of lucky talisman!

If my approach to parenting in the previous 17 years had tended towards laid-back, maybe slightly lackadaisical at times, then no one was more surprised than me to find myself developing into the very antithesis of what I would call 'healthy' parenting style.

'Helicopter' parenting is something of a new phrase, coming out of our obsession as adults that the world has somehow become a demonic and dangerous place for our kids, and therefore we must direct all our energies into constant worrying about the state of the world. The result is parents who are so over-protective as to practically hover over them, like a helicopter, watching their every move and waiting for some imagined disaster to occur.

Now I'm certainly not suggesting we shouldn't care about our kids, but I think that over-protectiveness is just as harmful potentially as neglect.

Why am I saying this? Because I can almost guarantee that at some point after your child's diagnosis, you will find yourself behaving in typically 'helicopter-ish' ways. It will sneak up on you.

It might start relatively innocently with a concern for welfare, even when no undue concern is necessary, such as asking your child if they're ok when it's reasonably apparent they are just fine, thanks very much.

In those early post-diagnosis days, you may find it hard to leave them alone, even for a few minutes, 'in case something happens'. You may feel like nothing will happen if you watch them constantly. However, diabetes doesn't really care who's on the lookout.

Let's explore this 'in case something happens' theory a little more. What could go wrong with diabetes? Well an awful lot it would seem in both the short and the long term (remember, if you're going to arm yourself with medical information then please only refer to the websites JDRF and Diabetes UK, or speak with your expert clinician).

In reality, usually there will be some degree of warning before anything truly life-threatening develops.

Let's take the following typical examples:

- **Hypos:**

Or, low blood sugar levels, typically less than 4mmol/L (70g / dl in the US)

In the early days of diagnosis, it's reasonably fair to say that your child will probably feel the symptoms of a hypo quite distinctly. Everyone is different in how they feel, but you may see your child become very pale, glassy-eyed, slow in speech, or not making a lot of sense – they may seem drunk (classic one, this).

They will probably be grumpy or even aggressive and may want to be alone. All of this is ok so long as they can treat themselves appropriately and quickly with glucose tablets, Haribos or a high sugar level drink such as a sugary sports drink, orange juice or cola.

Please do be aware that not everyone has the same level of hypo awareness, and this is particularly true the further into post-diagnosis. My daughter has experienced a couple of occasions where she was completely unaware until she nearly blacked out, that her levels were plummeting quickly. It's only happened the once so far, but it is worth mentioning so you can at least note for the radar.

So, what about the danger? Hypos only really become potentially tricky if left untreated, in which case it will become clear very quickly that something is wrong. Your child may convulse, or even lose consciousness and you will need to take over treatment by quickly administering a glucose shot.

If this happens, don't put anything in their mouth which would require swallowing or chewing as they could choke. If the treatment is ineffective within 10 minutes roughly, you will need to call an ambulance.

Even then it's possible to survive a bad hypo without treatment as the liver may kick out glucose stores in an emergency which will eventually bring the child round. They will be groggy and grumpy, and probably super hungry, perhaps for the rest of that day. You may find they don't want to do anything except sleep or rest.

Sounds serious, right? Well, yes it can be, but only on a rare occasion and to date with my daughter I think she's only had one occasion where she was even slightly close to passing out.

This is certainly no reason to follow your child round asking them if they're ok every 2 seconds, just in case they might be about to have a hypo. Fact is, they will probably have a few hypos a week. Everyone is different, and things can be especially tricky in the early days as they will be figuring out correct insulin dosage levels and gauging response each time.

Then, just when you think they've got it sussed, they grow, or hormones kick off, and the whole balance is unsettled again. It's pointless trying to figure out that the medical profession has no answers for, it's akin to juggling jelly is all I can say.

- Hypers:

The polar opposite of a hypo, where the blood sugar levels are too high (technically this means anything above 7 mmol/L or 240 mg/dl in the US).

In this scenario, you will probably see some of the pre-diagnosis symptoms coming back – they may be grumpy and tired, thirsty, visiting the toilet a lot. An inability to concentrate is a classic sign and this can be particularly troublesome to the teenager who is mid-way through A-Levels!

Hypers need to be treated just as much as a hypo, and sometimes this will mean an extra shot of insulin, or it could mean taking a walk outdoors to get some exercise and help to push the body into getting rid of the extra sugar. If left untreated for a long period of time (and this is also true for situations where insulin doses are missed or deliberately not taken as is the case with diabulimia) then it's possible that keto-acidosis will develop and your child could become unconscious and require urgent hospital treatment.

Again, what's the likelihood of this happening so regularly as to become a serious concern? Probably fairly low in usual circumstances unless your child is deliberately mis-managing their diabetes.

Regular hospital checks and just the very fact that they will feel like absolute crap if they don't treat themselves well should help to keep this life-threatening situation at bay. Of course, there are circumstances which could lead to DKA without any deliberate will, such as developing insulin resistance for example or infection or serious illness. However, your child will doubtless make it clear that they're unwell before anything too bad happens.

Both hypos and hypers are serious, don't get me wrong, but they're usually like the sell-by dates on food. Strange analogy but bear with me. Some people get freaked out by food that's a day past it's 'best before' date, presumably thinking that once the clock ticks past the hour of midnight, the food will suddenly become immediately toxic to the equivalent of a nuclear weapons arsenal. Not usually so, the food will continue to GRADUALLY deteriorate. It won't self-combust without warning.

Here's what you should remember about hypos and hypers – they can come on quite quickly but you will get some warning signs and symptoms most of the time and be able to do something about it before it becomes serious. It's not a case of 10 seconds in and you're dead as I could myself have imagined the first time I witnessed a full-blown hypo.

So, what to take from this?

You might read the above and be even more fearful than before. I sincerely hope not since I want to try to show you that even the most serious of immediate medical crises can be managed without too much panic.

At first, I could not sleep because I was scared that my daughter would die in her bed at night. That's normal but at the same time also irrational. It led me to the kind of warped thinking made 'real' by sky-high anxiety levels, to the point where I couldn't even think straight and it became such a massive 'thing' in our lives that no one could see past it or find a way through it.

This anxiety of mine fed from my thoughts into my behaviour, and then projected from me to my daughter, who then also started to become even more anxious about her condition.

The very opposite of my good intentions had become a reality and my daughter was starting to push me away, trying to keep her symptoms from me despite at the same time wanting to keep me close. My helicoptering had led to the very opposite of what it was 'supposed' to achieve.

Let's take another favourite of mine – the 'remote' surveillance via text, phone calls, social media monitoring.

I am ashamed to admit that I had developed stalker-ish tendencies which would come to the fore when my daughter was out on a night with her friends. Especially if alcohol was involved. Even on a day trip out where she wouldn't have adult supervision (and why should she, at almost 18!) it wouldn't be unusual for me to watch my phone like a hawk and then check in on social media to see if anything bad had happened, because obviously, no one would think to phone me if it had.... This hyper-vigilance meant that I could never switch off and relax unless she was right under my nose, literally.

The only time I felt a little more able to relax if she was away from me / home, was when she was at school (teachers would be able to look after her), or with her dad. Only then did I feel like she was with someone who would be able to do as I would if I were there. Writing this now, it feels a little bit control-freakery and I guess it was, however well-intentioned.

Just at a point in our lives when she had been enjoying the usual freedoms afforded to a teenager on the verge of being legally of age, the pot had tipped over and it was quite literally like having a new-born again. Emotionally that's how it felt. She was vulnerable and fragile and needed to be wrapped in cotton wool.

Except that she wasn't. She was doing great, managing her condition like a complete trooper. Taking it all in her stride.

Turns out it was me who was fragile and I couldn't hide this from her like a strong adult should.

What helped me to cope:

- Becoming as knowledgeable as possible about the condition so as to not over-imagine things which were unlikely to happen, physically. (this won't be helpful to everyone, but for me, knowledge is power).

- Talking to my daughter to understand more about how she felt about her condition, what plans she had in place to help her if needed (e.g. friends carrying spare kit). Letting her guide the conversation so she felt she could talk to me about her worries.

- Building a positive dialogue around Diabetes, rather than a negative one of worry and anxiety. For example, letting my daughter initiate the conversation and responding positively. Positive thoughts lead to more positive patterns of behaviour.

- Being kind to myself and recognising that I was going through a grieving process here.

a.   Impact on siblings:

If you don't have any other children, then by all means feel free to skip this section!

If, on the other hand, you do, then please read on...

My daughter has 2 siblings – twins who are 8.5 years younger. At the time of her diagnosis they were 9 years old.

This is quite a tricky age, for many reasons. Firstly, they are old enough to realise that something is wrong, but not necessarily old enough to understand exactly what diabetes is. However, it's definitely true that children tend to take things in their stride and have a grasp of many more situations than perhaps we give them credit for.

When my daughter was first diagnosed, the twins were there at the hospital with us, so of course they knew something was afoot. I don't remember explaining too much to them at the time, other than perhaps in general terms that their sister had been poorly for a little while, and was now getting the treatment that she needed. I made sure to keep the conversation upbeat and to focus on the positive for them (and for me, if I'm honest).

If you had asked them, I'm sure this wouldn't have come as a surprise anyway, since they had for sure witnessed their sister drinking loads and getting thinner, and had probably also overheard hushed conversations about potential causes over the preceding summer.

I'm not about to tell you how you should break the news and discuss the subject with your child, as you will know best of course how to do this.

Remember that just as you are feeling all sorts of emotions from denial, through to anger and guilt, they too will be reacting in their own unique way.

Much like when a new baby comes into the family, they may be feeling left out as all your attention is on the newly diagnosed child. They may feel jealousy, or anger, and may start showing their upset in hard to pinpoint ways.

Perhaps they start being reluctant to go to school (subtext: they want your attention too), or maybe they start acting up or lashing out in anger. All of these things are entirely normal behaviour, and depending on the age of your child and their emotional maturity, will need addressing in a way only you as a parent will know best.

For really young children, it might be a good idea to use a well-written picture book aimed at their age group to explain how diabetes works. (insert examples)

Older children might take comfort in a one to one with you to explain what's happening, or perhaps a family meeting depending on your own family dynamics.

Whatever their age it will be important for them to understand how to get help if their sibling is in trouble. They need to know, just as for any medical emergency, that they should find an adult quickly should the need arise. If that's the one thing they take away, then brilliant.

They may worry that their sibling will get sick, or be scared that they'll develop diabetes themselves.

Maybe you've changed the family routine, and this has resulted in a direct impact on them through changes to diet, removal of sweets and so on.

Their sibling might become more aggressive, emotional and maybe slightly unpredictable. They need to know why this might be the case and you need to help them to be as kind and understanding as possible. However, younger siblings may struggle to understand the mood swings and behavioural changes.

It's highly likely there will be jealousy as they may be feeling scared, lonely and confused with the focus and energy directed away from them.

Be aware of your own behaviour as a parent. Mums can often be the more emotional of the parent combination, and your own stress and anxiety may be changing your own behaviours, which your other children will doubtless pick up on.

Often as time goes on, you'll be surprised to find that your other children may become quite defensive of any misunderstandings among their peers about the difference between type 1 and type 2 diabetes[1].

They may well become mini ambassadors on behalf of their sibling, and will often be very protective of them!

Although life doesn't change completely, they will without doubt notice how their brother or sister has had to adjust to injections and taking blood as being part of everyday life.

It is clear parents play an enormous part in helping the undiagnosed sibling understand what is happening to their brother or sister.

---

1. https://jdrf.org.uk/about-type-1-diabetes/understanding/what-is-the-difference-between-type-1-and-type-2-diabetes/

However, it will hopefully be the case that that type 1 diabetes brings the whole family closer together, dealing with the condition as a team. This will include not only immediate but also extended family too and anyone close who regularly cares for the children.

a. Other people's opinions:

As a parent, having your child diagnosed with diabetes is a shock, and you need time to come to terms with this life-changing event.

You may well find that the practical side of dealing with the condition comes much more readily and quickly than the emotional sense of loss, grief and anger, which could take much longer to process and to reckon with.

As you begin to talk to others about the news, you will find that plenty of people have an opinion on how you should be dealing with things. Usually they are very well meaning (much like those who have an opinion on parenthood they feel compelled to share the minute you announce a pregnancy), but often misguided.

I've had people tell me I'm everything from 'hyper- sensitive' (well, thanks!), to 'practical', 'strong' and 'unflappable'. In truth, at the time it was said, the first comment was probably most accurate, though I can't say that hearing it didn't make me angry and tearful at the same time. Why on earth shouldn't I be 'hyper-sensitive' to a life-threatening condition? What inhuman robot wouldn't be? I can look back on that comment now from a more accepting and stable place, but I can't say it doesn't still sting.

People on the whole mean well, but often they don't get that their supposed nuggets of 'wisdom' they feel compelled to share with you when they hear the news, really aren't that helpful at all. In fact, they can be downright hurtful at a time when you as a parent are feeling particularly vulnerable and raw.

Let's be a little sympathetic - they probably know as much about type 1 as you did before your son or daughter was diagnosed.

Here are some real 'gems' you might well be on the receiving end of:

1. **At least it's not that serious:**

    Bite your tongue, if you can and say that yes, it's not a terminal diagnosis but it carries huge risks both short and long term, and can be life threating at any time if not properly managed.

1. **Perhaps you could try a change in diet:**

    If you're anything like me, you'll find yourself getting outraged at the confusion between T1 and T2. Try not to, after all, T1 affects only 400k people in the UK, way less than T2, so it's not surprising that when the media talks about diabetes it's usually the diet related T2 they're referring to.

1. **Maybe they might get better in time/ outgrow it:**

This is just plain wrong, but you can't blame people for not being a medical expert so maybe explain in brief terms that it's a lifelong incurable condition and leave it at that.

1. **It could be worse:**

Well of course, they could be dead. I mean what a ridiculous thing to say. Yes, there are probably 'worse' conditions / illnesses out there but it's never right to pit one against another.

1. **Should he/she be eating that?**

Again, probably confusion with Type2- you can't blame people for thinking that a diabetic shouldn't be eating sugar. I probably thought the same before I had any dealings with the disease. Type 1 diabetics are of course able to eat everything anyone else would, so long as accompanied by the corresponding level of insulin. And in moderation, the same advice as would apply for anyone.

1. **My Aunty Dot had diabetes:**

They're trying to be empathetic but it's impossible to compare one person's diabetes with another as everyone is different. What works for one person won't necessarily be right for another.

1. **How do they cope with the needles?**

I get super angry at this one. What do you say? Well, if they don't inject they die? Brutal but true. It soon stops people in their tracks that one!

Part 4: My final words of advice to you as a parent, friend, relative or carer:

This is only the start of our journey, and of course, none of us know what the future holds. I really hope that you and your family find some comfort and support in what you have read in this book.

Most of all, please remember the following words of wisdom and you won't go too far wrong:

- Your child's illness is not your fault – there is nothing that can be done to prevent type 1 from happening so don't beat yourself up about and the 'what ifs and maybes'.

- Don't waste your time on guilt and wishing you had done things differently –put your energy (and anger if you must) into working on a positive future.

- If people offer help, accept it with open arms and without judgement.

- Look after yourself both mentally and physically so you can be your best version for you, and your family.

- Don't neglect others who need you too.

- Use your knowledge to help others where you can.

- Talk to other parents of type 1s for both your own support and to lend support to someone who needs it.

- Make sure you have plenty of time where diabetes isn't dominating conversation – for both your sanity and your child's.

And remember, every life hurdle or event you navigate safely (their first sleepover, first night out, first trip abroad) is a massive learning curve and you will emerge from it stronger and more resilient than ever before.

With love and best wishes to you and your family.

Sara

CONTACT ME......

I hope this book has both inspired and helped you.

I'd love to hear from you, please email me at sara_hickmott@me.com or via my website at www.sarahickmottauthor.com[1] where you can also find a link to download your FREE bonus mini wellbeing collection:

VISIT THESE......

www.jdrf.org.uk[1]

www.diabetes.org.uk[2]

www.diabetes.org[3]

www.jdrf.org[4]

A BIG THANK YOU TO......

This book is dedicated to my darling daughter Ellie, the subject of my writings, to her single-minded determination to face her diagnosis head-on and to manage her life with diabetes as the inspirational and ambitious young woman she is proving to be. We are so proud of you.

Also to my long-suffering husband and to my beautiful twin son and daughter, who are as much a part of

---

1. http://www.jdrf.org.uk

2. http://www.diabetes.org.uk

3. http://www.diabetes.org

4. http://www.jdrf.org

this journey as me, and without whose support, love and understanding I simply could not function.

Love you all, always.

x

Don't miss out!

Click the button below and you can sign up to receive emails whenever Sara Hickmott publishes a new book. There's no charge and no obligation.

https://books2read.com/r/B-A-WFNF-IQWQ

Connecting independent readers to independent writers.

About the Author

Sara was born and raised in Hertfordshire, UK. A University of Leeds Alumni, Sara is a fluent German speaker, and loves writing books and blogging, foreign languages, swimming and running. She is a mum to 3 beautiful children and owns 2 lively dogs. www.sarahickmottauthor.com

Read more at https://www.sarahickmottauthor.com.

Printed in Great Britain
by Amazon